ONE BRIEF LIFE

Fifty Poems

JULIANA WHITTEN

Julie was my 6th, 7th, & 8th grade English, history, and drama teacher in Sausalito Public Schools. Julie had this unspoken in-tuned knowledge of identifying children who struggled emotionally. We developed an inspired instant connection. Julie has mentored and mothered me since I was a child, and she was also a good friend to the family. She and my mother Marie connected very well.

Although she knew something was terribly wrong with me, she never pried and I never had to tell. I heard the Lord telling me to go see Julie and get her to help me with my 20-year vision of writing a book, Alice N Crackland, which we worked on together for ten years. Julie cradled me as I told my trauma story of my life before I moved to California. She was a safe haven for me, and we shared many good laughs as well.

Julie has also touched the lives of numerous other Sausalito/ Marin City/Houseboat children who are now adults. She paid special attention to our academics, and showed commitment and devotion to our feelings. I am honored to write this forward regarding Julie's lifetime collection of poems that reflects the history of who she was and is, the journey she has traveled, and the many lives she's made a difference in.

- Author, La Wanda Marrero

Copyright © 2024 by Juliana Whitten
ISBN eBook: 978-1-963917-86-4
ISBN Paperback: 978-1-963917-84-0
ISBN Hardback: 978-1-963917-85-7
LCCN: 2025901394

All rights reserved. No part of this book may be reproduced or transmitted in any form or by any means, electronic or mechanical, including photocopying, recording, or by any information storage and retrieval system without express written permission from the author, except in the case of brief quotations embodied in critical reviews and certain other noncommercial uses permitted by copyright law.

Printed in the United States of America.

Table of Contents

Biography 7
Preface 9
Dedication 10
TRYING TO WRITE A GOOD POEM 11
THE LEAF 12
WHERE IS LOVE 13
THE WHEEL OF WHEAT 14
L'EAU ET LE CIEL 15
LET US DANCE ONE MOMENT 16
ALL THE WEIGHT 17
SUCH STRANGE AND WONDERFUL THOUGHTS AT 18 18
HAVE YOU/HAVE YOU NOT/ LOVED 20
GRAY, FIRST LIGHT, GRAY 21
CAN YOU SEE ME? 22
SO SO GOOD 24
THE SACRIFICE WE MAKE 26
THE BLACK CAT 27
ANOTHER BLACK CAT 29
SOMEWHERE OVER THE RAINBOW 31
RECOVERY 33
CHILDREN'S VOICES 34
JAN MIRIKITANI 35
BIG BILL MARTIN AND THE DANCE GROUP 37
JENNIFER KING, A PHENOMENAL WOMAN 38

Table of Contents

MONTHLY CYCLE: FERTILITY	39
MORNING	40
MOURNING THE LOSS OF CATHY TATE	41
MUSIC, MINDFUL	42
MOTHER'S DAY 5/97	43
HEAT WAVE	44
HAIKUS	45
GIVE US THIS DAY	47
DARK AND SHADOWS	49
ON HEARING SOME BAD NEWS ABOUT MY NEIGHBOR	50
THE VAGRANTS' VACATION	52
SLEEPING WITH MY TWO GRANDDAUGHTERS	53
AMERICA DIVIDED: RED vs BLUE	55
NIGHTMARE ON WALNUT STREET	59
BREATHING IN, BREATHING OUT	61
ALL THAT FALLS	63
DEATH IN THE SEAS	65
LOVING THE SKIN I'M IN	67
MY TIME IS SHORT	69
MY TONGUE LIES SILENT	71
OH, HAPPY DAY!	72
OH, MY HEART!	74
OLD AGE	77
ONCE A MAN, TWICE A CHILD	79
JUNE 7, 2023	82
INFESTATION	83
GOING THROUGH OLD LETTERS	84
AM I LIVING LIFE	86

Biography

I was born on June 7, 1942, in Des Moines, Iowa, a midwestern girl at heart. I was privileged in every way: my father was a renowned hand surgeon, my mother a community activist who put her family first. I had two older siblings and lived in a fine old house in a beautiful green neighborhood where I roamed freely.

My childhood world was rich with activities—I particularly loved summer camp in Minnesota. I was cheerful, accomplished, and anxious. I always wanted the two things in life that Freud said were important: to work, and to love. Oh, and I wanted to have fun AND make a difference along the way!

For work, I can say with pride that I was a Good Teacher. For thirty years in Oakland and Sausalito/Marin City, I taught large groups of bright, vulnerable, cynical, neglected, resilient children and teens to respect themselves, one another, me, and literary skills.

As to love, I married interracially and for seventeen years we enjoyed a diverse and culturally rich lifestyle in San Francisco and Berkeley. Because of my marriage my father "disowned" me, a harsh punishment indeed. Along with our village, I/we "raised"— well, maybe guided-- two biracial sons to be loving, responsible, creative, mostly ethical, funny, productive young men who know how to stay out of jail and contribute to the world.

In 1979 I co-founded I-Pride, the nation's second organization dedicated to the support and well-being of interracial families and multi-ethnic individuals. I have volunteered in countless organizations, such as Project Open Hand, Berkeley Youth Alternatives, Glide Church's Outreach, Options Recovery, Art Enables, Berkeley Repertory Theater, Arena Stage, Battered Women's Shelter, various women's groups, Stagebridge Storytellers, West Oakland Senior Center writing group, Course in Miracles, etc.

I have tutored young and old in writing, and co-authored two books. A scholarship called the Juliana B Whitten Hope Award was established in my honor as an educational grant. After teaching middle school, I mentored new teachers in districts throughout the Bay Area. I have written my life story in my poetry.

Now in retirement, I get to read voraciously, play tennis, eat adventurously, travel this beautiful, endangered planet, and spend time with my beloved grandkids in Washington, DC, my other "home." And I continue to work on the basic lesson of life: loving kindness towards myself and others, remembering we are all One, and in a blink, we'll be gone, or cycled into other magnificent forms.

Preface

I've been asked when I'm going to write my memoir
If you're curious to know the real me
You can read my poems
And I sincerely hope
You will find me there
And find yourself
And the world
Laid boldly bare
And beautiful.

Author's Disclaimer: *The following fifty poems were written between the ages of thirteen and eighty-two. They are not in chronological order. If they sound childish, adolescent, or middle/old aged, that's what they are. That's who I was/am.*
.
*   - J W*

Dedication

To my mother and father, Scripps College, and my beloved community Berkeley; together they gave me an array of tools for my life: confidence, curiosity, creativity, courage, conscience.

TRYING TO WRITE A GOOD POEM

With a frown

I'm sitting down

Let's see what words come marching, tumbling, rumbling

Out of my silent lips or fingertips or mental blips bumbling,

You'd think some fully blown deep thoughts might soon

Materialize, marshaled up in the dim wintry afternoon

Oh

No

It seems now the cold

And the old

Have delayed

Or frayed

Appearances, and we're left with clever useless fluff

And silence as marvelous as any eloquent or meaningful stuff

No form nor beat

Just rhymes, no meat.

Took a while,

But now I smile.

.

THE LEAF

The single leaf perches brightly
in the patch of sun
on my kitchen table like
 a green, yellow and brown
bird
it flew onto the deck
today in the deep yellow-green
of early August
 displaying all the stages
of its one brief life
 a time lapse photo
living and dying
perfect asymmetry
 a portent:
a few tiny brown spots
 of decay
(I have them too)
 the seeds of the end
 are always present
in the beginning.

WHERE IS LOVE?

Moth moon-dived.
Flowing molten
His limbs overcame me.

You cannot scribble me away
He said in my dream
And I awoke to the sound
Of his words in my head
And solitude.
I can never seem to get
the right balance of people
and myself.

All the world seems as empty and cold
As my arms.
Is love the life substance of the world?
These are the sentiments of young girls
At evening with peach skies
And no one to hold them.
Yet I feel older
A deeper longing
Than a tearful hope.
It is a hunger of my very soul.

I wait and am impatient in the waiting.
I long for the wilderness.
If I had a way and time
I would go
And cry where no one could hear me.

But I do not need that
I need a Self
Whatever that is.
Then I'll have love.

THE WHEEL OF WHEAT

The wheel of wheat harvest spinning
through the endless falls of time
hark to my agonies
 all torn and dark,
dying remembering the wind waving hills
amber waves of grain and chaff
 falling below the purple mountains
the high and empty skies
all the old country and bad dreams
all the baby-child girls and women
all the coming sorrows coming forecast and actual
 as if it were war or winter
and we were not all young and waiting
as if it were soon to thunder and snow
 as if I were not alone
 if only love
 without which
certainly
uncertainty.

L'EAU ET LE CIEL

l'eau est clair et bleu
le ciel est lourd et menaçant
le soir et le vent viennent
      doucement vers moi
et je pleure, sans confort
      toute seule.
Pourquoi le douleur?
Je ne dis pas meme a Dieu.

The water is clear and blue
The sky is low and threatening
The evening and the wind are coming
      gently towards me
And I cry, without comfort
      all alone.
Why so sad?
I am not talking even to God.

LET US DANCE ONE MOMENT

Let us dance one moment

And ponder the next

We are outer and inner —a saying

No more lyrical than hunger or peace, yet

Between the single acts

Fall the thousand shadows

Man must be both

(Himself, to himself and to them

And everyone's actor, to them and to himself).

Of courage, give me what there is

To spin in and out

As we bend time and infinity

And are bent

In this expanding and contracting

Universe.

ALL THE WEIGHT

All the weight of my young and many years

Settles down on me

This night, in this world

How finally alone we all are—

Another still point, and an outward look

At this strange world built around me

Gathered all around me:

The summation —arbitrary faith

Nothing inevitable

All is accident or choice, after all

We only rent our own houses.

SUCH STRANGE AND WONDERFUL THOUGHTS AT 18

I have such strange and wonderful thoughts.
I'm filled with such a burning and whirling desire for life.
Oh God, if I could only explain how I feel,
I think you would understand.

It is good to know I have my life clean and unfulfilled ahead of me.
I am eighteen and can never die.
Why can't I express the howling fury that chews inside of me?
Will I find the door, the face?
Who is the stranger in the mirror?
What is the point of the maudlin game?
      the insensate folly? the noble baseness of life?
I am the handler of my freedom, my own jailor.
I am the dealer of the cards, my own fortune teller.

I dread old age—the guilt of rocking chairs, the weakness,
      the humble unseeing eyes
remembering golden days that were only tin.

I want to be real, be free, be alive—
      then to die, quickly.

Passion, pain, pride,
    The hunger that grows from everything it feeds upon
    The thirst that gulps down rivers yet remains insatiate
    The hollow footsteps upon night's face,
    The long journey to reality, unreality, then death.
    I don't want my life to be futile.
    Will I have the courage to make it meaningful?
    Can I rise above the past and create
    Happiness?

                              - Julie Bruner   1960

HAVE YOU/
HAVE YOU NOT/
LOVED

Here, love
Wrapping me in bliss
Warmth and magical music
Then without warning   gone   you
Were folded into the universe's dark arms you
Evaporated into the ethers
Disappeared in a breath, a blink   I
No longer seeing you   listen for
And hear, here, hear   your echoes   ringing
All around and in me
So painful so empty
I want the real
You.

GRAY, FIRST LIGHT, GRAY

Gray, first light, beige,
Above, thick dark gray
Dim black silhouettes of trunks and branches

Soft peach
Pink, a sliver of blue beneath gray
Through the twigs

From a shaggy nest
Arise two little shadowy squirrels
Bolting down the tree

Below shining pink clouds
Tawny orange
Becomes a glowing crack

Suddenly, molten gold
Pours from the Y in the tree
Blazing fire lighting everything

A pattern of leaves bursts onto my curtains
Trees have turned to brown and thick
The dawn has become bright morning

Now, without warning
The light dims, pales, leaves,
A great gray curtain covers the promising day

CAN YOU SEE ME?

Cold dirty concrete

Under the freeway

Homeless tents and garbage

Cars racing overhead

Plastic bags flying

The pigeons pay no mind

But strut and circle

Dip and bow

Around one coy female

Plain gray

With little pink feet

She pecks and looks

And pecks and looks

While the guys

Fluff their glowing ruffs

Iridescent rainbows

Of male glamour

Stretch and bow

Circle and dance

Mutter and coo:

Notice me

Notice me

I'm fine

I'm big

See me?

See me!

But the gal walks away

They follow

Walks away

Follow and dance

Flies away

They follow

SO SO GOOD

Like me, she was a very good daughter
To her loving mother, and her overbearing father
Kind and thoughtful to a fault
"Miss Goody Two Shoes" we called her
A top A+ college classmate of mine
Eager, diligent, brilliant in class.

Unlike me, she was strong in her faith
Saying her rosary at night with her prayers
Together exploring our new independence
In the heady freshman days in our college dorm
Life without parents! but we were excelling, excelling
Surpassing good, to be better, to be best

Like all of us, she was exploring her body and its yearnings
With a friendly new boy, got carried away,
They didn't know anything about anything,
She lost her virginity and got pregnant
All in one swift fateful night!
really? really??
I was a good friend and, terrified,
drove her to her appointment. Waited, trembling.

Unlike her Virgin Mary, the fruit of her womb
Was not blessed, was cursed, rejected,
Brutally scraped from her young uterus

She was slapped awake in Tijuana's back alleys
And sent dazed and staggering back to the car.
Heart pounding, I drove across the border
While she, obeying her doctor's orders
Was sitting up, weeping,
Trying to look normal at the Mexican border,
Cramping, bleeding, and scared.

At her job in Disneyland that night
Bleeding, bleeding, blood dark as night
Down her legs, it wouldn't stop
She was wiping it up in the bathroom
Her face ghostly white.

Go to class, write papers, take tests.
A good Catholic girl mortally wounded
Living in grievous, grievous sin.
Infection set in. Hidden, untreated.
Don't tell anyone. Shhhhh.

Never able to conceive more babies
She married a rabbi, adopted a daughter
She was a good devoted mother
An illustrious actress in a famous company,
She relished that world of magic and make believe
Over the one where God's or Virgin Mary's mercies
Were so cruelly withheld.
She died young, still holding her dark secrets
Close to her unsuckled breasts.

THE SACRIFICE WE MAKE

He cut off his own foot so that

he might make the next leap.

She danced on the world, holding high

the banner of transformations.

He tore off his eyelids so that

he might see more clearly.

She sutured her lips so that

her soul could be heard singing.

THE BLACK CAT

In the past few weeks
Cats, everywhere, approaching me—
Sleek, bony, matted, glass eyed, strange
Cats coming up to me
From out of the bushes, around corners...
Now one out of nowhere, an unknown cat
A strange cat, thin, so thin, maybe starving
With dry short fur, dusty, black,
All black, "bad luck" they say?
Suddenly appears in our backyard
I get up, we move together, synchronized,
Both gliding through space
Pulled toward the back door
He dashes in ahead of me
How bold and aggressive he is!
Unruffled, purposeful,
Not unsettled by the baby's approach
I don't want the kids to touch him
I try to get him to go out
And he moves untouched by my kicks at him
Not intended to connect
And he knows it he stops in the doorway,
Turns, stares at me with cold eyes

I see a dirty string around his neck
We inhabit this moment together
A hot June afternoon back porch moment
I decide to feed him and go
To slice some lamb— two small pieces—
While he eats hungrily I get the scissors
And cut off his string
Have I made him more anonymous?
Or have I set him free
I pick up his skinny body and put him out
He goes a ways then circles, and sits
He looks at me heavily, then slinks forward
Trying to come inside again
I'm sitting on the top step after cutting his meat
A sharp knife in my hand
I think I would use it to kill him
Before I let him in again
I'm shocked by this grim instinct
Wonder where such a thought
Could come from, ponder,
Is he a powerful spirit, a lost soul
A message from the universe?
Or just a stray black cat
Marked by centuries of superstition
Toughened by hunger and abuse.

ANOTHER BLACK CAT

The new neighbor's black cat
Knows me now, comes over
Cautiously to rub and be rubbed
A handsome fellow, shy but curious
Missing a hefty piece of his left ear
Fur sleek and soft as a mink's
Inky and thick with winter's bounty
He weaves and ducks
Walking in circles clearly enjoying
The skittish pleasure of our encounter
Then in a flash
He lunges to bite me
I knock him with my elbow
And he recoils with flattened ears
And dilated pupils in his golden eyes
Ready to attack! I thought…
Or play?
All he did was half-bite my hand
Refusing my clumsy offer of affection
Or dominance, he might have thought

Whose language are we speaking?
He could have sunk those razor sharp teeth
Down to the bone
But instead, he merely gestured
Gave me a warning
That he'd had enough of my petting.
I admired the clarity and directness of his message
But now I'd had enough of him.
(I can't wait to see this bad boy again.)

SOMEWHERE OVER THE RAINBOW

Somewhere down the far distant
Corridors of my mind
I hear old songs:
Tunes, words, bits and fragments,
First they arrive unannounced
Humming and insistent strands
Furtive little rodents
Then I notice them,
Certain words repeating
(That's interesting)
Search for their meaning and message:
(Why that? Why now?)
Like a motherless child,
(today)
A long way from home
(Ah, right!)
You make me feel
You make me feel
Like a natural woman
(Last night)
Oh baby what you done to me
Make me feel so good inside
That old familiar
yearning, longing,
And I just wanna be
Close to you

Insistent ache,
Silent subscore
To my busy mother/teacher day
Or night,
Loneliness
In the soapy sponge, steering wheel, pillow
Maybe just a wishing
To be held, a lusting for a pair of arms,
Anyone's,
Hands, holding me
Fingers, in my hair...
Why then oh why can't I?
These images emerge, entwine and wrap
The tunes and words
"Stuck in my head"
Words without end
Worlds without end
Amen, amen.

RECOVERY

Serenity is seeping in
Soft
Gentle
Quiet
Palpable like an abdomen
Elusive
Warm like a child's back

I most notice it
In retrospect
And along the way too
This moment of fullness
This acceptance of things
I can and cannot change
Just me feeling good

This
Is what I'm here for
To do just this
Just now
Magnificent simplicity
Gratitude
Humility

God give me more
Times like these!
Your will not mine
I'm ready and steady
I'm proclaiming
I'm claiming
My highest good.

CHILDREN'S VOICES

Oh, I have heard them in my dreams! Every school yard

Has the sound of them, the shrill, the show offs, the sillies,

The warriors, the ones who demand to be heard, yelling

And whining and singing and screaming

It warms my heart, fills me up with nostalgic sentiments

(That is if I'm not tired or trying to relax

After a day in the classroom or yard duty).

I remember days, mornings especially

When my own children played in the back yard

Their voices singing and playing made me feel so glad, so rich

The sirens and growls and warbles of their fantasies

Was sweet, sweet music to this mother's ears.

JAN MIRIKITANI

Jan, my friend
Your fragile embrace is cool, dry,
Light, like leaves which hold fast to the branch
So as not to fall before their time

Your eyes are deep caves
Inviting me in and closing me out
Deep wells of tears, opening,
Bringing up silent sorrows in me

Your earthquakes release sulfurous springs of pain
Of wishes ungranted, darkness and nightmares,
A struggling and strangling
Like a voyeur I ease close

Stand spellbound as I witness
A woman's silent weeping, grinding of teeth
Doors slamming, wet pillows, barbed wire,
A small crumpled figure in a dark closet

I know her!
We cover our scars as best we can
Hands cover our ears and mouth
The darkness around our eyes holds our secrets

We say nothing to no one
We squat amidst our anger and fears
To rise ash-covered, wearing our weariness
Like old sagging underwear next to our skin

We dry our tears and each other's
As women have done since time can remember
Our sorrows are brief lifetimes we carry
We never forget.

BIG BILL MARTIN AND THE DANCE GROUP

Dear Bill, big, handsome, strong
The very image of masculine style
Competent, articulate,
Committed to decency
You have given us some
Sweet singing moments
When you opened like a flower
Allowed some tears
Shared some of your secrets
Laid out like presents on the bed
You know how to free, now and then,
Your womanly aspect
And connect us all more closely with
Our own male and female selves
Our shadowy other halves
Your vulnerability helps us
Come together into a whole.

JENNIFER KING, A PHENOMENAL WOMAN

Jennifer's not the only one,
but she's *our one*:
strong black queen in her power
as sweet and feminine as a flower
powerful voice and gentle hand
willing to take a moral stand
brilliant teacher of the arts
I've seen her touch the hardest hearts
she brings out the best in all of us
her criticism inspires openness and trust
as teacher/ leader she's no snob
she works long hours at her job
as well as for work she's known for play
for feet that dance and hips that sway
sometimes her poems tease and taunt
and lust and yearn and shock and flaunt
like life itself she's brave and bold
her art and heart will not grow old
here's to our Jen: applause and cheers
thanks for these many wonderful years
now go on and have some wine or beers
while we smile at the memories through our tears.

MONTHLY CYCLE: FERTILITY

The days of my cycle
Reach a high point,
A silent subtle climax
A two-day soaring of life energy
Upward into excitement
Darkness, throbbing
And intense physical need:
The flood
Draws deeply
From its source.

The bump test—
Bang your butt down
Ah yes, you now know
From which side
The ovum has popped
Floating
Ready and
Waiting.

The fingertip test—
A simple string bridge
Reveals the brief window
Molecules are aligned
Into tubes within tubes
Beckoning, yearning
Pathways wide open
Calling my slippery body
To creation.

MORNING

As each day begins
I open my eyes
The dim light is gray in my room
The things that I own
The curtains, my books
Are here with me inside my tomb.

It's cloudy outside
I know without looking
The sun is hidden from view
But it's glorious spring
A new day's arrived
And my life's too good to be true.

Outside it grows brighter
I rise from my bed
And heat up the water for tea
I offer my thanks
For another new day
Ripe with blessings for me.

MOURNING THE LOSS OF CATHY TATE

I cry/"Hello" to your empty chair

"Goodbye" to your smile and grace

The light in the world has dimmed since you've gone

But oh, I'll remember your face

A twinkle, a frown, eyes patient and kind

A courageous spirit, a brilliant mind.

9/25/18

MUSIC, MINDFUL

Warm white light of winter   sun
Over and around us   everywhere   timeless
Green translucence lifting   breaking
Roar of the sea   steaming soup
Distant misty memories   waves exploding
Mists showering fine sprays   rainbows
Coronas   fogs   regrets
My children play war   in the wet sand
I sit and watch   mindful
Mending, as mothers have done at seasides   ever
Since time and children began.

MOTHER'S DAY   5/97

sad, frantic mother
swimming as fast as the sea

womanly fiddle body
play me a hot goddess vision

sit by me here
incubate my egg girl

the beautiful waves
buoy me up and rising

to shine in luscious power
to keep on swimming

HEAT WAVE

How *can* it be spring if it's so damn *hot*?
They say it is May, but cool it is *not!*
If today was over one hundred degrees
Tomorrow will bring us down to our knees
The weatherman says all records were broken
It seems that the calendar has misspoken!

It's a "Save the Air" day
Which means stay inside
If you've no air conditioning
Pull your curtains and hide
Or dash to the nearest swimming pool
And stay under water if you want to be cool.

Global warming or random chance?
What is creating this unseasonal dance?
Poor Mother Earth is sweating and sad
With wild fires, tornadoes, and heat waves so bad
That old folks are fainting and moaning and dying
The grass and the babies are thirsty and crying

With sweat trickling down from my neck to my feet
I dread stepping outside into the street
I try to stay under the shade of the trees
As I look for an ice cream store, oh please,
This has been anything but a fun day!
Can I please have a great big hot fudge sundae?

HAIKUS

Gleaming moon tonight
My sweet mama is long dead
I wish I could cry.

Deep in the jungle
Orchids gleam in dark shadows
Red birds swoop above.

My back is so stiff
Children's teeth are falling out
How'd I get so old?

If I told the truth
The sky might crack and shatter
The sound of tinkling glass

Poetry is words
Squeezed out on cake like rosettes
From a silver tube.

In my dream a cart
Carrying a resting horse
Curled up inside.

No Parisian silk
Is as soft and silky smooth
As my baby's neck.

Eyes sparkle, mouth smiles
Can he be flirting with me?
Smile at me again.

Summer's finally here.
Let's go have some State Fair fun!
Finger licking screams!

In the morning sun
Single strands of cobwebs float
Life is passing by.

Has slavery ended?
Oh no, not here, no, not there
Slavery's everywhere!

Cruel masters rule
Selfish pompous billionaires
Hoarding all the wealth

GIVE US THIS DAY

I hold the beauty of this October

Morning cupped in my hands like my hot tea

The crystal air around me

Reverberates with birdsong, breakfast smells, and traffic

Clink of neighbor's spoon against dish

I hold my breath listening:

O that singing mocking bird, a musical genius

On the chimney next door

Riffing his improvisations like Thelonius or Miles.

Under my slippered feet on the flagstones

Red and brown maple leaves fade

Curl, shrink and dissolve

While small apples and new butter lettuce

Offer up their autumnal sweetness

An airplane passes over.

I am alone, but not lonely

I have all of today and more,

Those gone and those coming

A breeze passes through

As the sun climbs behind the redwood tree

I hear the boys are up.

I turn to go inside

To begin making breakfast,

Carrying the scent of this earth

The gifts of this particular place and time

With me into the house.

DARK AND SHADOWS

I would tear off my eyelids to see

What's before me

Everywhere dark and shadows

Coalesce in pools of pulsing blood

I cannot see

But feel without my hands

Spinning blindly around and around

Being sucked down into holes

Of imploding blackness

Is this a nightmare?

Is this the end?

ON HEARING SOME BAD NEWS ABOUT MY NEIGHBOR

No! No! No!
Three good reasons why
This shouldn't be happening
And their ages are one, two, and four, all boys
God, they need their mother
Like every one of us, a sweet mommy
To have and to hold
Body, scent, milk, warmth, smiles, voice, hands, eyes
The love that surrounds
And brightens the day and night
No matter what.

The vile cancerous growth
Has turned to stone in
Her small soft nursing mother's breast
And spread silently into her lungs and bones
For months she ignored it
She thought the lump was milk.
Why, God? Why?
Are you so callous?

How could you invent a more odious plan
That contains so much suffering and sorrow?
Where is the redemption in this? God?
The Buddhists believe
That the knife of suffering cuts away
The veils of grasping and desire
So that our souls reach a sublime state
Of pure enlightenment,

Yes, but do the little babies
Need to be without their mothers?
And their mothers without their breasts and hair?
Even God, a merciful god we are told,
Would say no, no, never.

THE VAGRANTS' VACATION

Two very convivial conniving thieves—
A voluptuous vacuous vixen named Violetta
And a violent vain Viet Nam vet named Vince
(She in a violet velour veil,
He in a vivid vermillion vest)
Drove their vintage Volvo van
Into the Vanguard Bank vault
And filched a variety of valuable Covid vaccines
Hoping to give themselves and their friends
The advantages of vigor and vitality, but no!
Instead he got a vapid vascular vertigo
And she got a vicious vomiting!
When discovered, they became victims of a vast,
     vehement, and vociferous public condemnation
As well as a vitriolic vilification
By vaxers and anti-vaxers alike!
"Wait! We're vaccinated!" they vocalized vivaciously,
And that evening, furtively leaving Vallejo
In their lavender vintage Volvo van,
They were overheard saying,
"Vamanos! Vamanos a Vegas!"

SLEEPING WITH MY TWO GRAND DAUGHTERS

They are so beautiful
Long lashes soft on round cheeks
Innocent and peaceful in their sleep
One on each side of me
Curly hair in my face
Legs thrown over me
A cloud of sweet sweat and bath soap
Wraps us in a damp embrace
Me and my two snuggle bunnies
Pure bliss
This is what I asked for…

Pretty soon I can't stand it
The heat is unbearable
The squirming and whimpers and kicks
Are driving me mad.
I struggle up from the puppy pile
And escape to the guest bedroom
Where I try to get some sleep
Knowing that the baby will probably
Bark and whine for a ba-ba

Waking her sister and me
In the wee hours of the morning,
And sure enough, she does,
I stumble down to the kitchen to prepare it
And then, I regret to admit,
I forgot to change her diaper
(I am so out of practice)
And by morning, my lovely bed
With its designer sheets
Is soaked down to the mattress
In a wide-radius puddle ...
And my lovely girls awake
To smelly tangled soggy sheets,
Another bubble bath
And more love and happiness.
Grandma is exhausted
And against her best principles
Puts cartoons on the television
While she scrambles the eggs
Washes the berries
And butters the toast.

AMERICA DIVIDED: RED vs. BLUE

Sarcasm, name calling, lying,
bitter vitriol towards each other?
we savor vicious rumors
knee-jerk contempt
can we give up the pleasure of outrage?
have you seen the red map with blue edges and spots?
can we ever again be friends?
one nation under God, indivisible?

What is it that binds?
a friendship, is it?
an open heart that can
weather the seasons
of plenty and drought?
or fire, the blaze of differences
the voracious mouth that consumes and spews?
or maybe ice that freezes and burns?
Just shut up, no, hushhhhh,
tone it down
can we listen to the hated Other?
even a toddler knows to be curious,
the gifts of why, why?
No one wants to hear your tired story
again, again,
trimmed and folded to fit your self-justification

"But I..."
doesn't fly.
I'd rather listen to the toilet flush
or the songs of spiders.
"But why?"
can melt hard into soft
shifting shadows scattering
after the heat,
some light
entwined in our common ancestry
we are embodied in the same celestial dust
nourished by the same green Mother

But America! "sweet land of liberty"?
Solve the riddle of Old Glory:
Where's the skunk in the red, white and blue?
The white stripe between the two parties,
the putrid Stink of White Supremacy.
"with liberty and justice for all"
has a hollow ring to it
a nasty stench
and a taste as bitter as ashes
that brings us to our knees
and to the streets.

We can raise our weapons
in war against each other
fight, foment, hate
fear, avoid, bemoan

Stop the Steal!
Hang Mike Pence!
we can string up gallows
storm the sacred capital
and bash in the windows
crush those trying to defend it
attack our elected lawmakers
trying to count our votes
while hiding on the floor

or! we can listen,
"Stop! children, what's that sound?"
trying to hear
before we speak, or ask,
we can remember,
or imagine
we are all the walking wounded
dispirited spirits wandering
the same weary world
feeling unheard, locked out and poor

listen, and hear each other's words
and! maybe we can sing our ancient anthems
loud, together,
lifting our souls above our combative heads
with our one endearing voice.
Yes, let's try, I say yes,
yes again, can we "all just get along,"
we can listen, then ask simple questions
How are you doing?

we can sing out and join in
"It's a beautiful day in the neighborhood,
A beautiful day for a neighbor,
Would you be mine?
Please won't you be my neighbor"?

can we ever?
can we be kind and respectful friends?
in this jaded and suffering world
called America, Amerika, or even Amerikkka,
You better stop,
Hey, what's that sound?
Everybody look, what's going down?

some lyrics by Mr. Fred Rogers and Buffalo Springfield, 1966

NIGHTMARE ON WALNUT STREET

One AM
Awakened from sound sleep I hear
The patter of feet in the night
Two devious grandchildren are up
Doing something in the dark
I turn on a light
Busted!
One is perched innocently on her bed
One is heading out the back door
What are you doing?
I'm just getting some socks
Who turned the TV back on?
I don't know
I'm gonna inflate my bed now
Oh no you're not
You'll wake the people upstairs
My neck hurts
Oh. Okay.
Get into bed now
And go to sleep

Will you?

Uh huh. Uh huh.

Sure.

Wide awake

The mean ogre

I snap off the light

Return to my bed

The house is dead silent.

BREATHING IN, BREATHING OUT

I am measuring out my life
not in coffee spoons
but in teabags and toilet paper
text messages and blood thinners
morning, evening,
breathe in, breathe out
tick-fucking-tock.

Moons and bright moons come and go
silvering the garden, the bathroom floor,
breaths and deep breaths come in, go out
how much is left of my allotment?
no real or metaphoric knee presses
on my privileged white neck
yet I can't breathe, I'm dying.

Alas, in the rooms, friends and family
come and go, here, there,
here, then gone
disappeared not for good
but now, and then, for ever,

one impossible truth my mind and heart
must learn to swallow
while trying to breathe
in, out, in, out.

My mind invents my memoir
my poems are my documentary
stories, truths, and half-truths that have shaped my life
details I will pick and choose to disclose, or not
people, events, real, imagined
crafted from memories or wishes or dreams
I'm waiting for the right time
to tell them, when I'm eighty,
or ninety, or ninety-nine, or now
or never, not now, not ever.
I'm still just learning to breathe,
creating my (extra)ordinary life
breath by miraculous breath
word by word.

ALL THAT FALLS

I turn my face to the heavens
As those who have come before me
Since before time began and I see
All the world's blessings come
Falling down on me…

Plum and cherry blossoms pink, white
Petal storms of blinding beauty
Fluttering in the spring winds
White clouds floating in the bright blue skies
Catching in my hair
Covering the grass and sidewalks and

Big drops of warm rain
Falling from the thick dark clouds
Wetting the sidewalks, turning the leaves
Lifting up the smell of blacktop and dirt
Air electric with the charge of the
Coming summer thunderstorm and lightning and later

Leaves drying, loosening their grip
On the glorious oaks cottonwoods aspens dogwoods maples
Autumn winds sending leaves flying
In circles and drifting down
Into crackling dusty carpets of reds,
Browns, yellows, and oranges and soon

The air is swirling
With wet and ice cold flakes of snow
Sticking to my lashes, fence posts,
Wintry black branches of trees
Turning into barren arms stretching up
In supplication and worship and

All the cold distant stars winking
Bright pinpricks of light
In the dark impenetrable skies
Grand gaudy moon step aside
It's the little sisters of the sun
That spark my tiny imagination but

The most wondrous gift
That falls and falls upon my grateful life
Is the blazing golden sunlight
Our celestial lifeline my trustworthy
Umbilicus to the sublime
More constant and loyal than the predictable moon.

How can I possibly conceive of and
Receive these many mysterious splendors
That give my life its particular joys?
I'm merely mortal, dumbstruck by these miracles, yet
Reveling in the comforts of each familiar season
That keep falling, unfailing, falling.

DEATH IN THE SEAS

A candle in a night of storms,
Blown back and choked with rain,
Holds longer than the mounting forms
That ride time's hurricane.

                             Maxwell Anderson

All living things eventually die
Oh yes, I know, I know!
I fear death only when I see
The reefs turn white as snow

A ghostly barren landscape lies
As far as the eye can see
The brightly colored fish are gone
How can we let this be?

Gone the brilliant yellow tangs
The rainbow parrot fish
The silver barracudas—
If I could have one wish

I'd pray we find a way
To stop this warming trend
The waters are acidic and hot
Our selfishness must end

What right have we to wipe out
Millenia of nature's art
Why can't we humans see
This really isn't smart?

I doubt we can reverse it
It makes me want to cry
I fear a world of dying seas—
It means we too must die.

LOVING THE SKIN I'M IN

Soft fuzzy wrapping of my old bones and blood
More like paper now than skin
You are the journals of my lifetime, so many
Days and years under the blistering sun

Constellations of spots that hold rich memories
Of sparkling waters and blazing blue skies
Ripples of wrinkles as beautiful as
The traces of wind over the Sahara dunes.

Thin, translucent, and melting, like rice paper,
My dying mother's skin was ripped open
By a careless nurse, who began to cry, while
My mom patted his arm and comforted him.

"Biggest organ in your body," they say of skin,
If you count up all the varieties of sensations
Possible from this silky coverlet rounding the body,
It's got the orifices beat, hands down.

Heat, comfort, pain, pleasure
Our first, and then, our last, feelings on this earth
Rippling through us, from birth to bedsores, yet
My skin blooms with blossoms, breezes, bees.

Oh so nuanced: the cat's purr, the fur,
The warmth, the waves, the rumble,
A lover's kiss, just the way you like it,
A baby's wet insistent hungry mouth--

Rhythmic, yes, the tap dance of life
Upon our celestial bodies, contradicting
The myth of our separateness,
Stoking the sacred fires of connection.

MY TIME IS SHORT

My time is short now.
We appear, then we disappear
Like water closes over a diver.
One year after a good teacher leaves
No one remembers her at the school.
Babies come out of nowhere
Old people slip away into oblivion.
We notice, then we forget.
My life has been very long.
The sand in the hour glass keeps dropping
I sense it has almost run out
Then Sisyphus flips it over
And returns to his rock and hill
Still keeping a watchful eye.

Oh let's remember a few of the beauties—
the pink vaginal lining of the shell's insides
the hard brassy shine of the water and sky: connected.
The bright gold iris of the cat's eye
The depth and surprise of a beloved poem
The singular voice of a cherished friend

Feathers, rocks, tea leaves,,
The things of this earth have
More magic in them than can be counted.

I hate to think of missing out
On all the beauties of the earth
And the glories of the sky
But most of all the love
I will miss, the love…
I received so much, from my birth,
Was wrapped in its soft folds
Bathed in it every day and night
Always tended, never wanting
Molded into being and doing and loving,
As a child, friend, lover, wife, mother, sister, grandma, crone
To this day I am swept along
In the warm river of love's interconnections.

MY TONGUE LIES SILENT

My tongue lies silent
Like a slab of sod
Upon a new grave.

I lie awake, still
As darkness
Bleeds into the light.

Alive in the tomb
Of my body
I sigh. I smile.

I turn. I wait.
The mystery is present in me
Everything that is

And has been me,
Memories, dreams, shadows,
The foreshades of tomorrow

Gather and rest in this
Moment out of time
Inside these blankets.

There is no voice nor ear
For this knowing
Yet it hums, it vibrates.

OH, HAPPY DAY! (NOT)

This day finally arrived!
Oh joy! Oh yes!
There is karmic law operating
There is order in
    the moral ethers
Former President Trump has been
    accused
    arrested
    arraigned
at last!
    Finally
Poor abused Lady Liberty
    is beginning
    to lift her head,
    remove her blindfold.

Alas! Father Time has
    dampened the gaiety
    dimmed the brief hope
Trump marches on gleefully
    towards the White House
    while America splits even farther apart!

Can he possibly delay or sidestep
    91 criminal charges?
    will we ever see him glowering
        from behind bars?
It seems there really are people
    "Above the Law"
Their oily pockets full
    of crooked judges
    and dirty money.
    Sorry Lady Liberty.
Goddamnit!

OH, MY HEART!

Be strong, my heart!
Sweet, sweet heart, sweetheart,
Toiling there in the darkness
Of my chest, pushing along
The endless flow of blood and breath~
On you, my heart, my very life depends
And I love you now, for your devotion
To all my sacred and profane pursuits.
I didn't always care, but now,
You are the apple of my eye!
I love you! Dear heart!

I place my finger tips gently on my thin veins
And feel the erratic throb and wobble.
I hear you're getting tired, my love,
All these years of giving and receiving back
Less than what you sent forth,
Depleted returns on your tireless investments.
Sisyphus with his shoulder to that infernal rock
We old folks never knew what we had in there
Until we're told it's almost gone.

You are a miracle, my heart,
How you emerged strong and rhythmic
From the primordial dust and soup
And formed yourself from plain old muscle
Into a many chambered Victorian mansion
Room leading to room
Then down the long hallways
And back up to the rooms
A haunted house of spirits
Blowing ceaselessly through the Silent Nights
And my bustling demanding days.

Always I've expected nothing less than perfection,
Yet now I am told you are fibrillating:
Struggling fluttering stuttering
Vibrating jolting shuddering
Syncopating elevating shimmying
Shaking quaking trembling
Shivering quivering convulsing...
So active! So wild!
When all you really need to do is
Stay steady, stay steady,
Calm down, slow down,
And work, and rest,
And work, and rest, and work, and rest
And on and on
Until your work is done.

And then it's done, that's it, that's all.
You're still,
My love, my sweet heart.

But as they say,
"And the beat goes on…"
Pulsations of life and death
Continue and continue
They carry on and carry on
And on and on…
Until they're still,
And chill.

An aged man is but a paltry thing,
A tattered coat upon a stick, unless
Soul clap its hands and sing and louder sing
For every tatter in its mortal dress…"
                    W B Yeats

OLD AGE

We wear our physical bodies
Like shabby underwear
Drooping, with holes,
Comfortable and sad.

We lose our shape
We hang loosely
On the frame that
No longer stands up straight.

Even the white bones
Are getting soft
Like old slippers
Run over at the heels.

New patterns emerge:
Grainy and mottled
Lattice and lace
Speckles and spots.

We rejoin the birds
Our hands curling
Quaintly contracting
Into claws.
We lose our hair
Except in places
We don't want it:
Chin, nose, ears.

Our teeth wear out
Begin to yellow
And slowly loosen
In our unstable gums.

Our feet betray us
Catching on cracks
Tilting us sideways
Pitching us down.

Our lungs get boggy
Heavy and soggy
Wheezy and breezy
Shorter of breath

The reliable old ticker
Sputters and flutters
Sometimes eventually
Shudders and stops.

But the *spirit!*
Oh, shining!
Growing stronger
Blazing brighter

Beaming its glow
Flashing from the depths
Lighting the shadows
Singing in the trees

Clapping its hands
Calling out poems
Waving from the windows
Of the house burning down.

"For beauty with her band
These crooked cares hath wrought,
And shipped me into the land
From whence I first was brought"

Lord Vaux Thomas

ONCE A MAN, TWICE A CHILD

I'm becoming a child again and I want my mama.
"Once a man, twice a child," said Hemby Senior in his nineties.
Sometimes I just want to crawl in bed under the warm covers
And close my blurry eyes and sleep.

Thick of waist and ankle, thin of skin,
I see my friends and family list and lean as they creep
Down the stairs one by one.

"Come back soon because I might be dead,"
Said my old friend Dorothy.
"I have that horrible disease, what's it called?"

Ailments, doctor's appointments, medications,
Lists of things to remember to do,
Only a few things "catch my interest" any longer.

Tennis, dancing, teaching, playing, reading books galore
Creating beautiful things like poems, photos, collections of shells
My life overflowed with activities and beloved people

Slow and fast dances and smoldering glances
Have faded into the dissipating mists of the past.
Lust, love, longing …companions, husband, lovers, kids,
Where did they all go? Off to their own destinies.

Love: the early morning cool green freshness
The melancholy gold of the dropping sun
The pale blue sky of a quiet afternoon.

Like: the deep yellow yolks of the pasture raised eggs
The sweet juicy pulp of a fragrant orange
A slice of toasted baguette dripping salty butter.

Hate: the politics of war, the weeping bitter eyes
The injured dusty children dug out of the rubble
Arrogant big-money politicians justifying the carnage.

Meanwhile spring keeps insisting on popping into view
Tiny new pale green baby leaves waving before winter has gone
Daffodils below, magnolias above, blossoms along the streets.

And another familiar friend, or scary stranger
The dreaded Big C, unnamed, rhymes with Dancer,
Has fallen into step with me, spinning me around
On this quickening path toward my divine destiny.

I only want my mom (or someone) to hold my hand
And reassure me it will soon be okay
While I stumble fearful and brave along the way.

And now, a few days later, surgery is over,
My lymph glands are clean, my cancer's gone
All I have to do is get healed, get stronger, live.

I bask in the great good fortune of my luck
Revel in the knowledge that for now I'm getting healthy
and the consuming fire in my belly will slowly die out.

Patience, invisible, quiet, wait, and wait, and breathe,
The cells are slowwwwly mending, stitching, birthing
In that miracle of invention, healing, the ultimate reward.

June 7, 2023

Eighty-one means a great deal,
   physical pain stabbing my shoulder, my back
      and complete spiritual freedom, ease, peace, joy!
         in the small everyday things: clean clear water, my soft bed,
            81—a job well done! so far, so good, not over yet,
               so far, and farther to go…

Drawing my inspiration from nature, the birds, fresh flowers,
   my kids, books, my art, my poetry, my garden, tennis, dear friends,
      "my, me, mine," my private world to wonder about, to cherish!
         these things make me open my eyes every morning,
            dream every night…

Family, friends, and neighbors cheer me, connect me
   to feel safe, loved, blessed, cozy, happy, and yes, privileged,
      and vulnerable, isolated, hopeless, lonely, helpless, declining!
         waiting for some disastrous fall that will plummet me
            into *old* old age.

Eighty-one is a curse and a blessing,
   my story nearing its end, or not, perhaps just random events,
      or a meaningful unfolding of a mysterious Divine Order!
         wrinkled old lady careening along as both driver and passenger,
            excited about the next chapter, and the last
               glorious mistakes and adventures.

INFESTATION

moths
tenants
clothes
rugs
anxiety
disagreements
rights
needs
responsibilities
fears
poisons
pests
vacuum
strength
choices
conflict
research
beliefs
decisions
spray
money
wait
okay
breathe
clear
good
Wait!
what's
that
nasty
bugger
no!

GOING THROUGH OLD LETTERS

The old woman sits in the kitchen and weeps.
She is reading a letter from her mother (long-dead)
Sent to her at camp in Minnesota
When she was away for the summer.
She hears her mother's cheerful voice
Rising from the yellowed onion skin typing paper:

July 16, 1954, Well Sweetheart, the cat is ailing.
She just produced five ugly kittens.
The homeliest she has ever had!
Why doesn't she pick a good-looking father?
Daddy has moved them into the turkey box.
Your brother has a new girlfriend, Jennie.
The weather is blistering hot.
Please return the blue bathing suit.
I sent you a box, paper, and string.

The old woman remembers sunbathing on the dock
By the rippling lake, reading her mother's letters,
Listening to the call of the loons from the nearby island.
She was too busy riding horses and paddling canoes
To return the unwanted swimsuit.

She feels thirteen again as she reads the tender closing:
LOVE* LOVE* LOVE* LOVE*
She is so moved by the sparkle of those four little stars
As if they had arrived that morning.
Her throat tightens with tears.

She misses her mother.
She weighs the passage of half a century,
Feels she understands her mother better
Now that she has been a mother too
She wishes her children would call her more often
Or live closer.

AM I LIVING LIFE?

am I living life
or is life living me

life flows in me then one day stops
or when I stop, it keeps on going

the river picks up bodies along the way
then drops them as it goes, flows

a drop a pool an eddy a fall
a mist rising to disappear

clouds birds buds babies
everything blooms wilts falls disintegrates

appears ah!
disappears oh!

how does the river of being
pick us, use us, discard us

who am I really
what's my true name

when and why
where does it start

is there an ocean where it ends
a leaf leaves, leaves don't

flow flow
ever onward

life? death?
spirit? breath?

the planet's skin
ripples and wrinkles

how does life get into us
how does it leave out of us

do we magically spark into it
from some mysterious nowhere

is there a somewhere
where we return to from here

I feel it, I feel life!
my life pulsing

In and out
around about

I feel my living life!
slowly leaving

or is that just the river
freeing me?

Juliana Whitten and her grandson.

www.ingramcontent.com/pod-product-compliance
Lightning Source LLC
LaVergne TN
LVHW041713060526
838201LV00043B/706